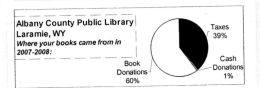

The
language
of
flowers

TEXT   **DESIGN**

◆   ◆

Diane Wallis   *Karen Carter*

First published in the United Kingdom in 1992 by Bookmart Limited.
Mill Hill Industrial Estate
Desford Road, Enderby
Leicester LE9 5AD

by arrangement with CollinsAngus&Robertson Publishers Pty Limited,
Sydney, Australia

First published in Australia in 1992 by
CollinsAngus&Robertson Publishers Pty Limited (ACN 009 913 517)
A division of HarperCollinsPublishers (Australia) Pty Limited
25-31 Ryde Road, Pymble NSW 2073, Australia

ISBN 0 207 17572 1

Cover photograph: Andre Martin
Internal photography: Andre Martin
Printed in Hong Kong

5   4   3   2   1
96 95 94 93 92

THEY SPEAK

NOT OF TORMENT

NOR BLACKNESS

NOR SIN.

flowers

QUIETLY AS

ANGELS COME

DO THE FLOWERS

COME IN.

ACANTHUS ◆ *fine arts*

AMBROSIA ◆ *love returned*

ANEMONE ◆ *sickness*

APPLE BLOSSOM ◆ *preference*

ASPHODEL ◆ *my regrets follow you to*

the grave

AZALEA ◆ *temperance*

BLUE BELL ◆ *constancy*

BORAGE ◆ *bluntness*

BROOM ◆ *neatness, humility*

BUTTERCUP ◆ *childishness*

CAMELLIA JAPONICA ◆ *unpretending*

excellence

He loves me

He loves me not

He loves me

CARNATION

◆

bonds of affection;

pure love

HYACINTH

◆

constancy

To see a World

in a Grain of Sand,

And a Heaven

in a Wild Flower,

Hold Infinity

in the palm

of your hand,

And Eternity

in an Hour.

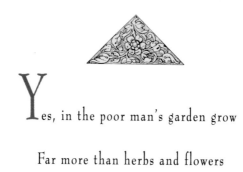

Yes, in the poor man's garden grow

Far more than herbs and flowers

Kind thoughts, contentment, peace of mind,

And joy for weary hours.

L A V E N D E R

◆

distrust

CARNATION, STRIPED ◆ *refusal*

■ CHRYSANTHEMUM, CHINESE ◆

cheerfulness under adversity

CLEMATIS ◆ *mental beauty*

■ CYCLAMEN ◆ *diffidence*

DAFFODIL ◆ *regard*

■ DAHLIA, SINGLE ◆ *good taste*

DAISY, DOUBLE ◆ *participation*

■ DANDELION ◆ *oracle*

DAPHNE ◆ *painting the lily*

■ FORGET-ME-NOT ◆ *true love*

FOXGLOVE ◆ *insincerity*

■ FUCHSIA ◆ *taste*

GERANIUM, ROSE OR PINK ◆ *preference*

■ GLOXINIA ◆ *a proud spirit*

HONESTY ◆ *honesty, sincerity*

I wandered lonely as a cloud
That floats on high o'er vales and hills
When all at once I saw a crowd,
A host, of golden daffodils;
Beside the lake, beneath the trees,
Fluttering and dancing in the breeze.

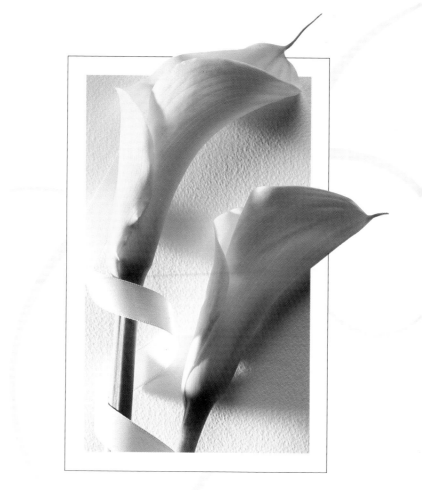

ARUM LILY

◆

purity

WEARING

THE

WHITE

FLOWER

OF A

BLAMELESS

LIFE

Through brakes

of the cedar

and

sycamore bowers

Struggles the light

that is love

to the flowers.

VIOLET, BLUE

◆

faithfulness

A VIOLET BY A MOSSY STONE

HALF HIDDEN FROM THE EYE!

— FAIR AS A STAR, WHEN ONLY ONE

IS SHINING IN THE SKY.

HONEYSUCKLE ◆ *bonds of love*

HYACINTH, BLUE ◆ *constancy*

IRIS ◆ *message*

JASMINE ◆ *amiability*

JONQUIL ◆ *desiring a return of affection*

LANTANA ◆ *rigour*

LAVENDER ◆ *distrust*

LEMON ◆ *zest*

LILAC, PURPLE ◆ *first emotions of love*

LILY OF THE VALLEY ◆ *return of*

happiness

LOBELIA ◆ *malevolence*

LUPIN ◆ *voraciousness*

MAGNOLIA, LAUREL LEAVED ◆ *love of*

nature

MARIGOLD ◆ *grief, despair*

MICHAELMAS DAISY ◆ *afterthought*

22

JONQUIL

desiring

a return

of

affection

R O S E

◆

love

O MY LUVE'S LIKE A RED, RED ROSE,

THAT'S NEWLY SPRUNG IN JUNE.

O MY LUVE'S LIKE THE MELODIE,

THAT'S SWEETLY PLAY'D IN TUNE.

P O P P Y

◆

consolation

But pleasures are like

poppies spread

You seize the flow'r,

its bloom is shed;

Or like the snow

falls in the river

A moment white,

then melts for ever.

I R I S

◆

message

You forgot

the flowers,

I have kept them

in a jar of water.

It smells as if

you're here.

S W E E T   P E A

◆

departure
and
lasting pleasures

H

O

P

E

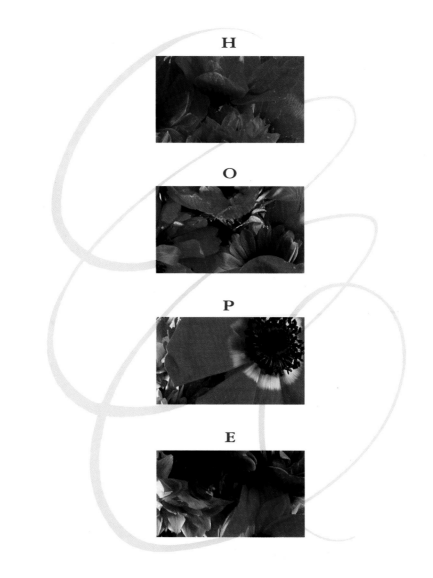

HOPE

IS THE THING WITH

FEATHERS

THAT

PERCHES

IN THE

SOUL,

AND SINGS

THE TUNE

WITHOUT

THE WORDS,

AND

NEVER STOPS

AT ALL.

DAISY

◆

*I share
your
sentiment*

*B*uttercups and daisies,

Oh, the pretty flowers;

Coming ere the Springtime,

To tell of sunny hours.

The rain

MOCK ORANGE ◆ *counterfeit*

MIMOSA ◆ *sensitivity*

falls upon

MORNING GLORY ◆ *affectation*

NARCISSUS ◆ *egotism*

the earth

NASTURTIUM ◆ *patriotism*

ORANGE BLOSSOMS ◆ *bridal festivities, purity, loveliness*

and grass

PANSY ◆ *thoughts*

PELARGONIUM ◆ *eagerness*

and flowers

PETUNIA ◆ *never despairing*

PHLOX ◆ *unanimity*

TULIP

◆

beautiful eyes

ROSE, PALE YELLOW

◆

Decrease of love,
jealousy

Life is a waste

of wearisome hours,

Which seldom the rose

of enjoyment adorns;

And the heart

that is soonest awake

to the flowers

Is always the first

to be touch'd

by the thorns.

39

And 'tis my faith that every flower
Enjoys the air it breathes.

Nature's first green is gold,

Her hardest hue to hold.

Her early leaf's a flower;

But only so an hour.

Then leaf subsides to leaf.

So Eden came to grief,

So dawn goes down to day.

Nothing gold can stay.

Too quick despairer, wherefore wilt thou go?

    Soon will the high Midsummer pomps come on,

Soon will the musk carnations break and swell,

    Soon shall we have gold-dusted snapdragon,

Sweet-William with his homely cottage-smell,

    And stocks in fragrant blow.

HERE
TULIPS
BLOOM
AS
THEY
ARE
TOLD;
UNKEMPT
ABOUT
THOSE
HEDGES
BLOWS
AN
ENGLISH
UNOFFICIAL
ROSE.

POLYANTHUS ❧ *pride of riches* ❧ POPPY, RED ❧ *consolation* ❧ PRIMROSE ❧ *early youth or sadness* ❧ RANUNCULUS ❧ *radiant with charms* ❧ ROSE ❧ *love* ❧ SNOWDROP ❧ *hope* ❧ STRAWBERRY BLOSSOM ❧ *foresight* ❧ SWEET PEA ❧ *departure and lasting pleasures* ❧ SWEET WILLIAM ❧ *gallantry* ❧ TUBEROSE ❧ *dangerous pleasures* ❧ TULIP, RED ❧ *declaration of love* ❧ VERONICA ❧ *fidelity* ❧ VIOLET, BLUE ❧ *faithfulness* ❧ WALL-FLOWER ❧ *fidelity in adversity* ❧ WATER LILY ❧ *purity of heart* ❧ WISTERIA ❧ *I cling to thee* ❧ ZINNIA ❧ *thoughts of absent friends* ❧

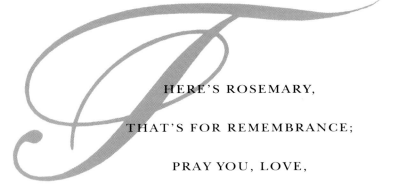

HERE'S ROSEMARY,

THAT'S FOR REMEMBRANCE;

PRAY YOU, LOVE,

REMEMBER.

AND THERE IS PANSIES,

THAT'S FOR THOUGHTS.

PANSY

◆

love; courtship

Therefore, on every morrow, are we wreathing

a flowery band to bind us to the earth.

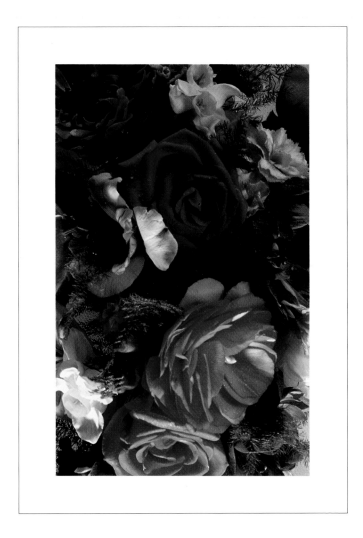

Shall I compare thee to a Summer's day?

Thou art more lovely and more temperate:

Rough winds do shake the darling buds of May,

And Summer's lease hath all too short a date.

Flowers
— *worthy of* —
Paradise

Spring, Spring, beautiful Spring,
Laden with glory and light you come;
With the leaf, the bloom, and the butterfly's wing,
Making our earth a fairy home.

'In most gardens,' the Tiger-lily said, 'they make the beds too soft — so that the flowers are always asleep.'

Sources

The verses and lines featured in *The Language of Flowers* have been taken from the following works:

page 4 From 'Flowers in the Ward', by Shaw Neilson

page 8 Anon

page 11 From 'Auguries of Innocence' by William Blake (1757-1827)

page 12 From 'The Poor Man's Garden' by Mary Howitt (1799-1888)

page 15 From 'I Wandered Lonely as a Cloud' (1807) by William Wordsworth (1770-1850)

page 17 From 'Idylls of the King' by Alfred, Lord Tennyson (1809-1882)

page 18 From 'Bellbirds' by Henry Kendall (1839-92)

page 21 From 'Poems founded on the Affections, VIII (Lucy)' by William Wordsworth

page 25 From 'O my Luve's like a Red, Red Rose' by Robert Burns (1759-96)

page 27 From 'Tam O'Shanter' by Robert Burns

page 29 From *Robert Gray Selected Poems* 1963-1983

page 33 From 'Hope' by Emily Dickinson (1830-86)

page 35 From 'Buttercups and Daisies' by Mary Howitt

page 36 From 'Rain' by William Carlos Williams (1883-1963)

page 39 From 'Oh! think not my spirits are always so light' from Irish Melodies by Thomas More (1779-1852)

page 40 From 'Lines written in early Spring' by William Wordsworth

page 42 From 'Nothing Gold Can Stay' by Robert Frost (1874-1963)

page 45 From 'Thyrsis' by Matthew Arnold (1822-88)

page 46 From 'The Old Vicarage' (1915) by Rupert Brooke (1887-1915)

page 50 From *Hamlet* Act Four, Scene 5, by William Shakespeare.

page 53 From the opening lines of 'Endymion' by John Keats (1795-1821)

page 55 From Sonnet no. XVIII by William Shakespeare

page 56 From 'Paradise Lost' by John Milton (1608-74)

page 59 From 'Spring' by Eliza Cook (1818-89)

page 60 From *Through the Looking Glass* by Lewis Carroll (1832-98)

BIBLIOGRAPHY

Harvey, G. (ed), *Poems of Inspiration and Comfort*, Avenel Books, New York, 1990.

Penguin Dictionary of Quotations, Penguin Books, England, 1981.

Penguin Modern Poets 9, Penguin Books, England, 1968.

Pickston, Margaret, *The Language of Flowers*, Michael Joseph, England, 1968.

Robert Gray Selected Poems 1963-1983, Angus & Robertson, Australia, 1985.

Selected Poems of Robert Frost, Holt, Rinehart and Winston Inc,. New York, 1963.

The Centuries' Poetry 3, Pope to Keats, Penguin Books, England, 1942

The Centuries' Poets Vol. 3, Penguin Books, England, 1942.

The Poems of Henry Kendall, Angus & Robertson, Australia, 1920.

The Poems of Shaw Neilson, Angus & Robertson, Australia, 1965

Williams, W.C, *Collected Poems*, Carcanet Press Limited, United Kingdom